한글

TEACHING SOUNDS

흔들이

한글 - Teaching Sounds

ISBN: 978-0-359-70444-6 (Paperback)

For information contact:
http://www.hundli.com

Book and Cover design by Taemin Kim

First Edition: October 2019

Contents

Preface

Most writing systems do not convey the science and logic beyond speech sounds. Unless educated, people cannot come into their full intelligence. On behalf of King Sejong the Great, the author writes 한글 concisely and completely based on its phonetics. He truly wishes that all people not only learn it easily but also practice scientific reasoning every day.

The Corean[1] alphabet, or Hangul, has obtained the highest recognition among all writing systems because of its scientific design. King Sejong the Great invented and promulgated Hunminjeongeum (Right Sounds to Teach People) in 1443 and 1446. Beyond the letters and sounds, it explains rich design principles from both phonetical and philosophical angles. But, the vowels' phonetic principles are less complete than the consonants'. Hangul, therefore, does not come into its own value in the world.

---

[1] Corea has been used for a long time and it is still used in many places. The author prefers it to Korea because it gives a neo-classical impression to the revisited Hangul completely based on the phonetics.

This book sums up the teachings in Hunminjeongeum into a scientific paradigm and completes the phonetics of Hangul, helping learners acquire Hangul efficiently and effectively. The author suggests that learners master fully the syllables in Section 1.2 and primitive letters in Chapter 2 marked by an asterisk (*). The syllables are easy to speak and learn. The primitive letters are a few and distinct, so learners may grasp and practice speech and graphic syllables from the start. With this base, learners will be able to master the more complex letters and sounds more efficiently.

This book uses the International Phonetic Alphabet (IPA) for phonetic transcriptions. For those who are not familiar with the IPA and articulatory phonetics, an interactive web application that presents speech sounds and their articulations of Hangul can be found at http://learnhangul.org. Hangul letter design in Section 1.3 marked by a dagger (†) may be complicated at first. If so, skim it through and come back later for deeper understanding.

Hangul is the epitome of the use of scientific reasoning to build visible, organized, rigid, and discrete things distilled from veiled, chaotic, transient, or vague processes. Sejong the Great in the 15th century exercised science and logic with the utmost ingenuity, formulating a phonetic writing system that resolved the communication and educational problems. It is amazing and inspiring that the design principles of Hangul had aligned altogether seamlessly, converged towards science's move in the 20th century, and still unravel missing puzzles and hidden codes in the 21st century.

1. Hangul Design

Hangul letters are tied completely with articulatory features of their speech sounds. Both vowel and consonant letters are designed by pictographic, derivative, and composite principles. The pictographic letters outline their speech organs' shapes or motions with dots, lines, and basic shapes. The derived letters add a diacritical dot or line for additional phonetic features. Composite letters combine the pictographic or derivative letters.

Hangul acquisition in practice is to learn the trilayered transformation between the phonetic processes and graphic symbols (Figure 1). Note that a syllable is the minimal phonetic unit of a word regardless of the language. In the top level, we want to transform over a thousand syllables back and forth between their sounds over time and letters on paper. To facilitate this, we can break down the syllables into smaller speech sounds in the middle level. Here it is very crucial that Hangul is a phonetic alphabet in which a letter has only one speech sound. Furthermore, we can organize the speech sounds by their phonetic features and design their letters orderly to have the graphic features. A few phonetic rules and primitive letters thus enable us to achieve trilayered Hangul acquisition in a short period of time.

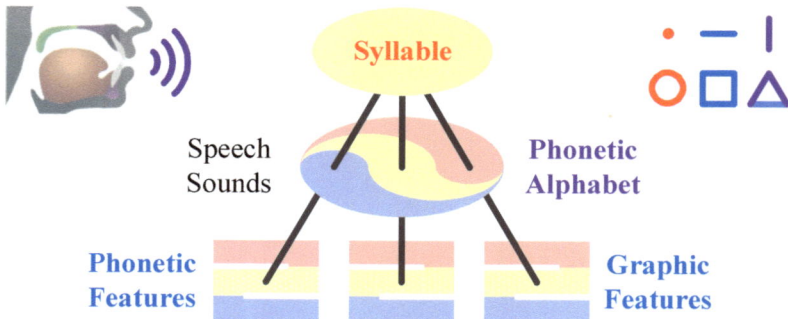

Figure 1. Hangul. Hangul acquisition is to learn the audiovisual transformation between phonetic processes and graphic symbols in three layers.

Hangul Wing is the periodic table of speech sounds and their letters that recapitulates the trilayered Hangul learning (Chapter 5). The speech is like organic substances by chemical analogy; syllables, speech sounds, and phonetic features are molecules, atoms, and atomic features, respectively. The syllable is a stable building block of a word as a component of speech. A syllable consists of speech sounds while a molecule consists of atoms. The periodic table of elements characterizes atoms by their number of valence electrons. Likewise, Hangul Wing organizes all speech sounds by their phonetic features that are encoded by graphic features of their letters.

1.1. Hundli Theory

Hundli theory, or Hundlism, outlines the world by its unity, diversity, and inclusion. In the world, a process starts, grows, and ends while the reality embodies basic, derived, and composite things (Table 1). The process and reality are not separable in that they describe the same world differently. Hundlism thus captures the holistic, multilateral, and inclusive world.

Table 1. Hundlism. Hundlism depicts the trilayered process and reality.

World / Primitives	Process	Reality	Sign
ᄒ [hʌn] (Round Sky)	Diverging	Derivative	<
이 [i] (Erect Men)	Binding	Composite	=
르 [dɯl] (Flat Earth)	Converging	Base	>

Hun·dl·i, a compound word of ᄒ [hʌn], 르 [dɯl], and 이 [i], means the world primitives in Corean (Figure 2). The first syllable, ᄒ, meant one and is the retro version of 한 [hɑn] that means great. The sky or sun is a good

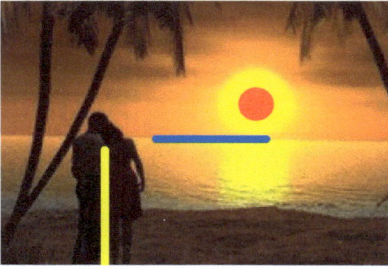

(a) World Primitives   (b) Samtaegeuk Pattern

Figure 2. World Primitives. (a) The world primitives include the round sky, flat earth, and upright men over the dot and lines (Background Image Credit: https://abstract.desktopnexus.com/wallpaper/74481/). (b) Samtaegeuk (literally three primitives) pattern represents the world primitives.

example that embraces those meanings in the world. It is a symbol of the derived thing or diverging process. The second syllable, 늘, means the flat earth, a symbol of the basic thing or converging process. The third syllable, 이, means a person or thing, a symbol of living things in harmony, which represents the binding or balance of 흔 and 늘. The three world primitives embody the harmonic dynamics of incompatibles.

The simplest geometric symbols include a dot, lines, and basic shapes that represent the world primitives (Table 2). The dot, horizontal line, and vertical line outline the most primitive and distinctive features of Hun, Dl, and I, respectively (Figure 2a). The basic shapes including a circle, square, and triangle also outline the distinctive shapes of the primitives. According

Table 2. Geometric Symbols vs. the World Primitives. The simplest geometric symbols include a dot, lines, and basic shapes (circle, square, and triangle).

World Primitives	Sky	Earth	Man	Letter Primitives
Dot & Lines	•	—			Vowel Letters
Basic Shapes	◯	□	△	Consonant Letters

to Information Theory, it is the more simple symbols that encode the more important things. Therefore, the dot and lines denote the primary letters for vowels and the basic shapes denote the secondary letters for consonants.

The Hundli pattern visualizes the incompatible duality and harmonic integrity of the world. It depicts the harmonic dynamics of two opposites coming from one substance as a process or reality (Figure 3). Despite there being diverse things in the world, Hundlism starts from the belief that the world is one (Figure 3a). Out of many, two is the least number that shows the largest contrast of the changing things in the world (Figure 3b). The Hundli pattern splits the boundary between two incompatibles in blue and red to show the one substance in the yellow background (Figure 3c). The red, blue, and yellow pieces represent Hun, Dl, and I, respectively. Two different fish violently chasing each other in the common pond overlay the subtlety between commonalities and differences in the world.

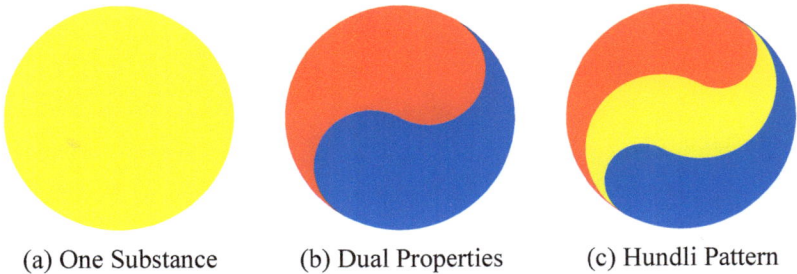

(a) One Substance   (b) Dual Properties   (c) Hundli Pattern

Figure 3. Hundli Pattern. (a) The yellow circle characterizes the unity of the world. (b) The one bears two opposite things in blue and red that interact with each other. (c) The Hundli pattern splits the boundary of the two to remind us that both come from the one substance in the world.

In this regard, other patterns mislead us about the world. For example, the Yin Yang pattern depicts the world by two incompatibles (Figure 3b). It gives us an atomic impression that the world is more competitive. The

Samtaekeuk pattern with three identical lobes gives us a similar impression that the world consists of equally independent primitives (Figure 2b). Both, however, fail to convey the harmonic aspect of the world explicitly.

The spiral Hundli pattern envisions the cyclic and nested structures as well. In the universe in yellow, the diverging Hun in red emerges outward (or upward) vigorously while the converging Dl in blue retreats inward (or downward) steadily. The cardinal directions align with the sign convention of the Cartesian coordinates and right-handed writing on paper. Between Hun and Dl, I in a yellow swift curve characterizes the agile, flexible, and harmonic properties of the living things. The yellow background displays the dual illusion of its branching and binding roles. Other Hundli patterns include tumbling, lying, and rectangular ones (Figure 4).

(a) Tumbling Hundli   (b) Lying Hundli   (c) Rectangular Hundli

Figure 4. Other Hundli Patterns. Tumbling, lying, and rectangular Hundli patterns give us diverse impressions, keeping the harmonic feeling.

In its dual sense of process and reality, Hundlism gives a fresh insight into the articulatory phonetics and design principles of Hangul. First, the graphic syllable on paper straightforwardly follows the trilayered structure of the speech syllable over time (Section 1.2). Second, letters and sounds of the syllables manifest the bilateral and trilateral structures in symmetry (Section 1.3). Hundlism thus condenses the phonetic and graphic designs of Hangul into the trilateral process and reality in the world.

1.2. Speech and Graphic Syllables[*]

A speech syllable is the minimal phonetic unit of a word and it consists of opening, lasting, and closing sounds. The speech syllable forms, lasts, and diminishes over time as it is mechanically analogous to the noise caused by one cycle of an acoustic valve. The swing valve on the pipe produces three types of air noise (Figure 5). (a) The squeezing airflow produces an opening sound when the valve is opening. (b) The running air produces a lasting sound when we keep the valve open. (c) The choked airflow makes a closing sound when the valve is closing. In the vocal tract, an articulator controls the airflow from the sound source to produce its opening, lasting, or closing sounds. For example, "mom" [mʌm] contains the three sounds as the mouth opens, sustains, and closes. The lasting sound is often called a vowel while the opening or closing sound is a consonant.

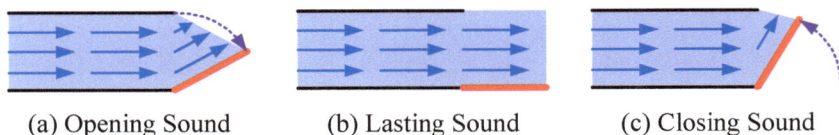

(a) Opening Sound   (b) Lasting Sound   (c) Closing Sound

Figure 5. Opening, Lasting, and Closing Sounds. (a) The opening valve produces the opening sound. (b) The opened valve produces the lasting sound. (c) The closing valve produces the closing sound.

We can transform a syllable back and forth between its speech syllable over time and graphic syllable on paper (Figure 6). On the vertical axis, we speak opening, lasting, and closing sounds of a speech syllable (Figure 6a). Accordingly, their respective letters are placed at the top (ᶜO), middle (–|), and bottom (O⸃) in a graphic syllable (Figure 6b). Here O and –| denote an arbitrary consonant and vowel letter, respectively. O's angle brackets distinguish between the opening and closing letters. This syllabic template

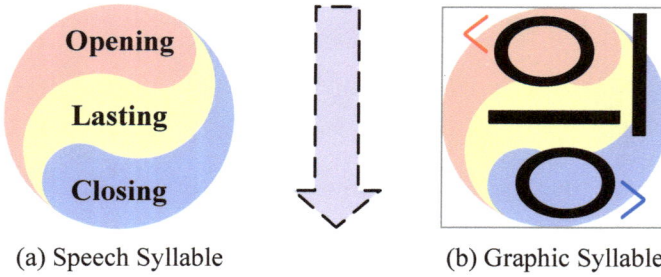

(a) Speech Syllable   (b) Graphic Syllable

Figure 6. Trilateral Speech and Graphic Syllables. (a) A speech syllable consists of opening, lasting, and closing sounds over time. (b) Accordingly, a graphic syllable places opening, lasting, and closing letters at the top, middle and bottom, respectively, in a syllabic block.

is named 잉 [iŋ] or simply wing. The trilayered graphic syllable supports all writing directions and it is particularly optimal for vertical writing.

The lasting sound is essential in a speech syllable while both opening and lasting letters are essential in a graphic syllable. If an opening sound is silent, ○ is placed in ⁵○. ○ₔ is omitted if the closing sound is silent. Fat, tall, or big vowels containing ─, │, or both, respectively, occupy the area beneath, to the right, or both places relative to ⁵○.

1.3. Letters and Sounds[†]

In the trilayered syllable, letters and sounds are counterparts, organized in parallel by trilateral structures. The speech sounds are classified as basic, derivative, or composite ones; their letters are designed respectively by the pictographic, derivative, and composite rules in general. Thus phonetic and graphic complexities of a letter and syllable correspond to each other. Note that the composite sound consists of more than one simple sound while the basic and derivative ones differ subtly. The pictographic letter outlines its articulator's shape while the derivative and composite ones differ subtly.

Several distinctive features make up the simple vowel and consonant charts completely (Figure 7). First, the mouth opening, lip puckering, and tongue height span the simple vowel chart (Figure 7a). For example, the full, half, quarter, and minimal mouth opening with plain lips make [ɑ], [ʌ], [ə], and [ɯ], respectively. Additionally, lip puckering makes four different sounds. Second, binary occlusion, aspiration, and tensity for vocal valves span the consonant chart (Figure 7b). For example, the aspirate version of [ɯ] is [h]. But, not all possible sounds are effective in the Corean language.

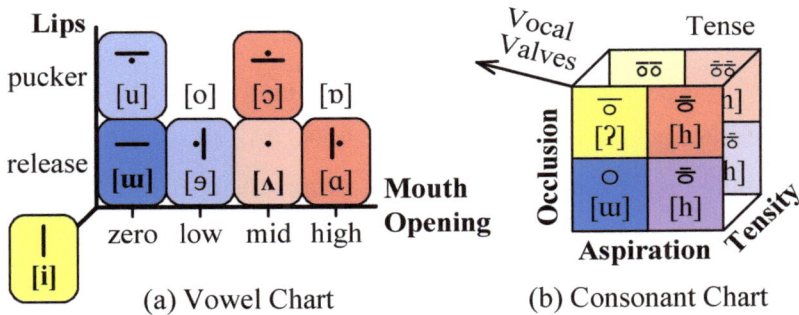

Figure 7. Vowel and Consonant Charts. (a) The lip puckering, mouth opening, and tongue height span all simple vowels. (b) The binary occlusion, aspiration, and tensity span the simple consonant chart.

Several articulatory features compactly make up alternative vowel and consonant charts (Figure 8). First, the palatal movement and tongue height span the alternative vowel chart (Figure 8a). The palatal movement aligns with the phonetic qualities of babies' cooing sounds: [ɔ], [ɑ], [u], [ə], and [ʌ]. Second, several articulators, tertiary airflow, and binary tensity make up the alternative consonant chart (Figure 8b). The articulators include the lips, teeth, tongue, and throat (Figure 10a). The tertiary airflow replaces the binary occlusion and aspiration. For example, the sound sources with low and high airflows produce [ɯ] and [h], respectively.

9

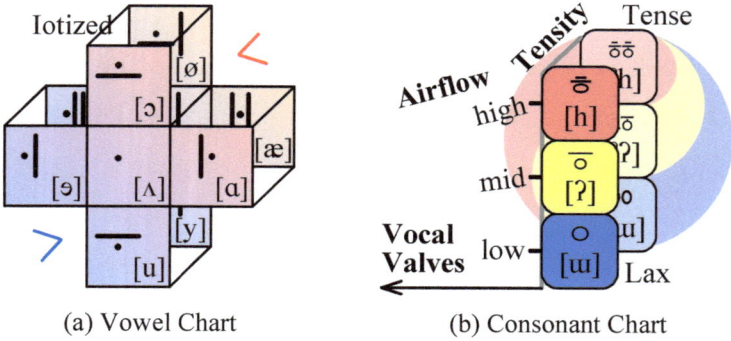

(a) Vowel Chart   (b) Consonant Chart

Figure 8. Alternative Vowel and Consonant Charts. (a) Phonetic quality and tongue height span most simple vowels. (b) The places and manners of articulation, airflow, and tensity span all consonants.

Intuitive and orderly changes in Hangul primitives and letters help us grasp their underlying principles (Figures 9 and 10). By a cosmic analogy of the mouth, a dot and lines outline the round palate, flat of the tongue, and raised tongue back as articulatory features of the primitive vowels (Figure 9a). The palate is the roof of the mouth. Coincidently, 하늘 [hanʌl] meant sky as well as palate around the 15th century in Corea. In a sense, the flat tongue is the bottom of the mouth. Thus, the tongue back is raised between the roof and bottom of the mouth. By another cosmic analogy of

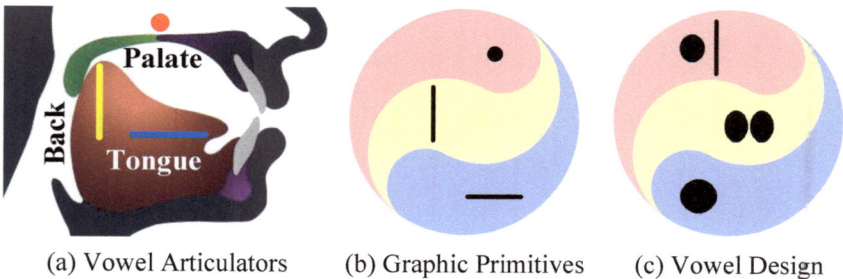

(a) Vowel Articulators   (b) Graphic Primitives   (c) Vowel Design

Figure 9. Vowel Geometry and Formation Processes. (a and b) The dot and lines outline the round palate, flat tongue, and raised tongue back. (c) The vowel letters from pictographs bear derivatives and composites.

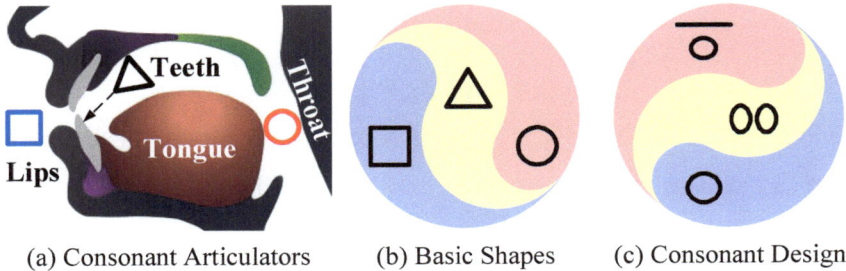

(a) Consonant Articulators   (b) Basic Shapes   (c) Consonant Design

Figure 10. Consonant Geometry and Formation Processes. (a and b) The basic shapes outline the lips, teeth, and throat in the articulatory profile. (c) The pictographic consonant letters bear derivatives and composites.

the mouth, the basic shapes outline longways the exhaling throat, lippy air vessel, and sharp teeth for the primitive consonants (Figure 10a).

The pictographic, derivative, and composite letters are designed by the dialectic rule of Hundlism for Hangul vowels and consonants in symmetry (Figures 9c and 10c). Here a solid circle (or expanded dot) and hollow circle denote arbitrary vowel and consonant letters, respectively. Both from Hun in Figures 9b and 10b turn into the pictographic bases on Dl in Figures 9c and 10c to seed the Hangul formation process. For the vowels, a pictograph (●) bears its derivative letter by adding a dot or line (●|) to it and a composite letter combines two letters (●●). Note that ●| for [i], as a graphic syllable, reminds us of the iotized vowel, where the dot and line are the diacritical marks for pre-iotized and post-iotized vowels, respectively. For example, ㅗ and ㅏ are pictographs. ㅑ and ㅐ are two iotized vowels of ㅏ. ㅗ and ㅐ compose ㅙ. For the consonants, a pictograph (○) bears its derivative letter (ㅎ) putting a line on it and a composite letter combines two letters (○○). For example, ㅎ and ㅎ̄ is the first and second derivatives of ○. The double letter of a lax sound denotes its tense sound.

2. Primitive Letters[*]

The dot, lines, and basic shapes outline the primitive articulators for their speech sounds that compose the primitive syllables. In particular, the dot and lines are mapped to the primitive vowels while the basic shapes to the primitive consonants. The combination of three primitive opening, lasting, and closing sounds results in the twenty seven primitive syllables.

2.1. Primitive Vowels

The primitive vowels include [ʌ], [ɯ], and [i] whose active articulators are outlined by the dot and lines (Figure 11). First, the dot (•) symbolizes the vibrant palate when the central [ʌ] is produced at the half mouth opening (Figure 11a). Second, a horizontal line (—) outlines the flat tongue vibrant when the flat [ɯ] is produced at the minimal mouth opening (Figure 11b). Third, a vertical line (|) depicts the tongue back raised when the free [i] is produced at the minimal mouth opening (Figure 11c). The vowel letters are located in the central region of the graphic syllable (Figure 12).

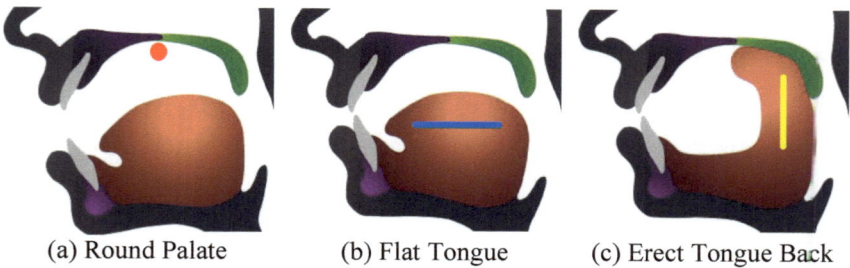

(a) Round Palate   (b) Flat Tongue   (c) Erect Tongue Back

Figure 11. Primitive Vowels. (a) • [ʌ] symbolizes the round palate. (b) — [ɯ] outlines the flat tongue. (c) | [i] outlines the erect tongue back.

The primitive vowels base diverging, converging, and iotized vowels (Chapter 3). • [ʌ] is the average cooing sound for most babies. — [ɯ] is the plainest sound source that highlights the adjacent speech sounds. • [ʌ]

11

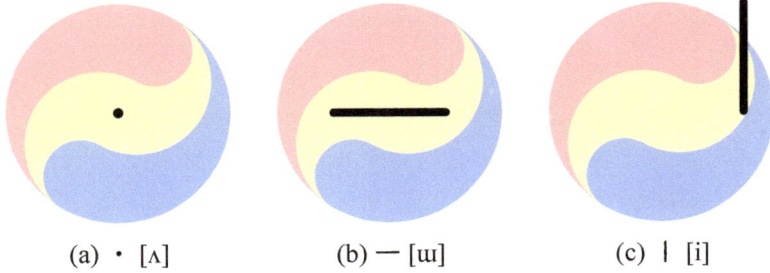

(a) · [ʌ]   (b) — [ɯ]   (c) | [i]

Figure 12. Primitive Vowels in the Syllabic Block. (a) A dot is placed at the center. (b) A fat vowel is placed horizontally in the middle. (c) A tall vowel is placed rightward but still in the central region.

and — [ɯ] are diverging and converging references, respectively, to define their secondary vowels whose letters combine · with — or | . Lastly, | [i] derives the iotized vowels whose letters add · or | to the base letters.

2.2. Primitive Consonants

The primitive opening sounds include [m], [s], and [ɯ] that the square, triangle, and circle outline the lips, teeth, and throat (Figure 13). Despite our preoccupation with silence for ○, soft airflow from the throat with no tension produces the "throaty" sound [ɯ] (Figure 13c or 11b). The opening lips from Figure 13a to 13c produce the "lippy" opening sound [m] by es-

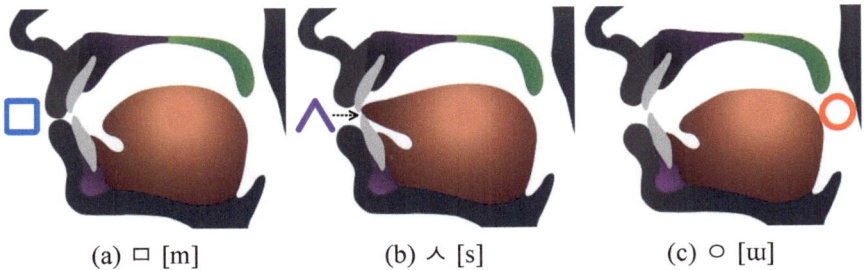

(a) □ [m]   (b) ㅅ [s]   (c) ○ [ɯ]

Figure 13. Primitive Sounds. (a) □ [m] oulines the square lips. (b) ㅅ [s] outlines the sharp teeth. (c) ○ [ɯ] outlines the round throat.

caping air through them. With the tip of the tongue, opening teeth from Figure 13b to 13c produce the "toothy" opening sound [s]. Their opening letters are placed at the top of the syllabic block (Figure 14).

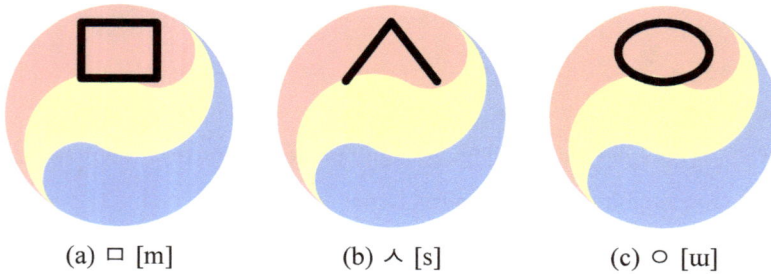

(a) □ [m]   (b) ∧ [s]   (c) ○ [ɯ]

Figure 14. Primitive Opening Letters. A square for [m], triangle for [s], and circle for [ɯ] are placed at the top of the syllabic block.

Remarkably, the primitive opening sounds have important phonetical properties. First, the throaty sound is swallowed by other adjacent sounds and often considered as a silent placeholder since it is identical to — [ɯ]. This articulation defines the reference state where an opening articulation ends and a closing articulation starts. Second, the lippy sound is the easiest and most conspicuous one that a baby can babble for the first time. Thus baby words meaning mother or food contain this sound in most languages. Third, the toothy sound is voiceless while the first two are voiced.

Simply, reverse the opening articulation, if possible, and it will define the closing sound whose letter reuses its opening letter placed differently in the syllabic block. When we are closing the oral tract, a choked airflow produces the closing sound. First, the closing lips from Figure 13c to 13a produce a nasal sound, that is, the closing [m], due to escaping air through the nasal tract. Second, the closing teeth from Figure 13c to 13b block the oral tract airtight by the tip of the tongue that makes the closing [t]. Third, the throat itself cannot close the vocal tract, so its closing sound is silent.

The closing sounds are distinct from their opening sounds, but placing the opening letters at the bottom of the syllabic block makes it unnecessary to create an additional letter or diacritical mark for them (Figure 15).

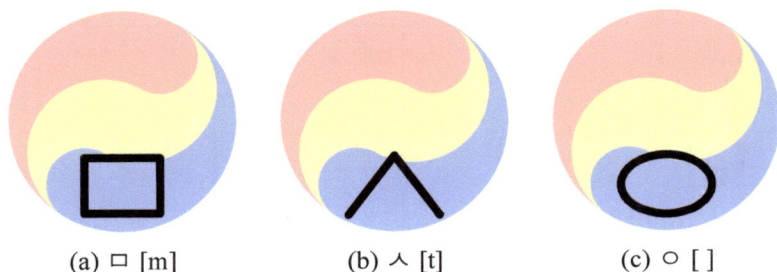

(a) □ [m]   (b) ㅅ [t]   (c) ○ [ ]

Figure 15. Primitive Closing Letters. A square for [m], triangle for [t], and circle for [ ] are placed at the bottom of the syllabic block.

The primitive consonants represent all consonants and their phonetic properties as their articulators can open and close the oral tract (Chapter 4). First, □ [m] represent nasal sounds whose first and second derivatives make the same closing sound. Those sounds are maximally distinguishable as their articulators open and close the oral tract by themselves. Second, ㅅ [s] and its derivatives are voiceless and have the same closing sound [t] as the teeth can open and close the oral tract with the tongue tip. Third, ○ [ɯ] is the twice differentiable sound source that cannot close the oral tract. ○ denotes a basic letter distinguished from the derivative and composite ones.

2.3. Primitive Syllables

The primitive opening, lasting, and closing sounds compose twenty seven primitive syllables. First, the primitive opening and lasting sounds form the (three-by-three) nine primitive open syllables (Table 3). Accordingly, their syllabic letters place primitive opening and lasting letters at the top and middle, respectively. In a sense, ○ at the bottom is simply omitted as

Table 3. Primitive Open Syllables. The full combination of opening and lasting sounds compose nine open syllables.

			Opening / Lasting
□ [m]	∧ [s]	○ [ɯ]	
□ [mʌ]	∧ [sʌ]	○ [ʌ]	[ʌ]
□ [mi]	∧ [si]	○ [i]	[i]
□ [mɯ]	∧ [sɯ]	○ [ɯ]	[ɯ]

Table 4. Primitive Rhymes. The primitive lasting and closing sounds compose six primitive rhymes: three rhymes for closing □ and ∧.

			Lasting / Closing
[ʌ]	[i]	[ɯ]	
□ [ʌm]	□ [im]	□ [ɯm]	□ [m]
∧ [ʌt]	∧ [it]	∧ [ɯt]	∧ [t]

its closing sound is silent. Second, the primitive lasting and closing sounds compose six primitive rhymes: three lippy and three toothy rhymes (Table 4). The rhyme letters place one primitive lasting and one primitive closing letters at the middle and bottom of the syllabic block, respectively. Note that they are not legitimate graphic syllables. Third, the primitive opening sounds and lippy rhymes make nine primitive lip-closed syllables (Table 5). Fourth, the primitive opening sounds and toothy rhymes also make nine

Table 5. Primitive Lip-closed Syllables. The primitive opening sounds and lippy rhymes compose primitive lip-closed syllables.

[m]	[s]	[ɯ]	Opening / Rhymes
[mʌm]	[sʌm]	[ʌm]	[ʌm]
[mim]	[sim]	[im]	[im]
[mɯm]	[sɯm]	[ɯm]	[ɯm]

Table 6. Primitive Tooth-closed Syllables. The primitive opening sounds and toothy rhymes compose primitive tooth-closed syllables.

[m]	[s]	[ɯ]	Opening / Rhymes
[mʌt]	[sʌt]	[ʌt]	[ʌt]
[mit]	[sit]	[it]	[it]
[mɯt]	[sɯt]	[ɯt]	[ɯt]

primitive tooth-closed syllables (Table 6). Note that the IPA transcribes a consonant differently for its opening and closing sounds. For example, [s] and [t] denote ㅅ's opening and closing sounds, respectively.

Hangul letters are named by their closest speech syllables to remind us of their speech sounds. First, the vowel letter is named simply by its sound as a complete syllable. The name in the graphic syllable adds ㅇ at the top as in the third column in Table 3. Second, the consonant letter is named by the closest syllables to its speech sounds (Table 7). With the indistinct ㅡ [ɯ], the first and second syllables manifest its opening and closing sounds, respectively. For example, 므음 for ㅁ, 스읏 for ㅅ, and 으 for ㅇ. The disyllabic name contracts to one syllable having ㅡ [ɯ] between the opening and closing sounds. For example, 믐 for ㅁ and 슷 for ㅅ.

Table 7. Primitive Consonant Names. The consonant letter is named by its opening and closing sounds with ㅡ [ɯ] contractible to one syllable.

Primitive Consonants	ㅁ [m]	ㅅ [s]	ㅇ [ɯ]
Consonant Names	므음 [mɯ.ɯm]	스읏 [sɯ.ɯt]	으 [ɯ]
Monosyllabic Names	믐 [mɯm]	슷 [sɯt]	으 [ɯ]

Unlike linear writing systems, opening and closing sounds of the same letters are clearly recognizable by their places in Hangul graphic syllables. Typographically, unbalanced syllables can be adjusted for a better look. In particular, open syllables are often expanded to fit in a syllabic block. For example, ㅁ, ㅅ, and 으 elongate the standard ones in the last row of Table 3. The syllable break is intuitively obvious in Hangul. The period (.) marks the syllable break in the IPA (Table 7).

3. Vowel Letters

All vowel letters are combinations of dots and lines. The pictographic vowels characterize their articulators' shapes or phonetic qualities. Raising the tongue back derives the iotized vowels whose letters add a dot and line to the base letters. The composite vowels blend two vowels in harmony.

3.1. Pictographic Vowels

The pictographic vowels assort into the primitive and secondary ones. The primitive vowels include · [ʌ], — [ɯ], and | [i] that outline the palate, flat tongue, and erect tongue back, respectively, as described in Section 2.1.

The secondary vowels include [ɔ], [ɑ], [u], and [ə] whose letters with a dot and line reveal their phonetic qualities (Figure 16). They are distinct from each other in most languages: [ɔ] is an expression of awe (firing up), [ɑ] is a shouting sound (feeling outward), [u] is a booing sound (feeling down), and [ə] is a filler word (feeling inward). Accordingly, their letters' dot orientation tells us their phonetic qualities: upward ⊥ [ɔ], outward ⊦

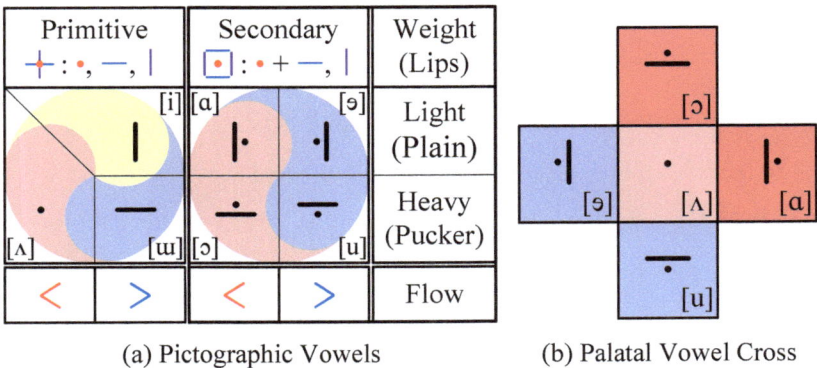

(a) Pictographic Vowels   (b) Palatal Vowel Cross

Figure 16. Pictographic Vowels and Vowel Cross. (a) The pictographic vowels include three primitive vowels and four secondary vowels. (b) The secondary vowels around · [ʌ] form the palatal vowel cross.

18

[ɑ], downward ㅜ [u], and inward ㅓ [ə]. On the one hand, mouth opening and lip puckering contrast their flow and weight in the secondary vowel square (Figure 16a). On the other hand, their phonetic qualities form the palatal vowel cross (Figure 16b). In fact, these palatal vowels with one dot cover the full spectrum of babies' cooing sounds. The primitive opening and secondary lasting sounds compose twelve open syllables (Table 8).

Table 8. Secondary Open Syllables. The three primitive opening and four secondary lasting sounds compose twelve open syllables.

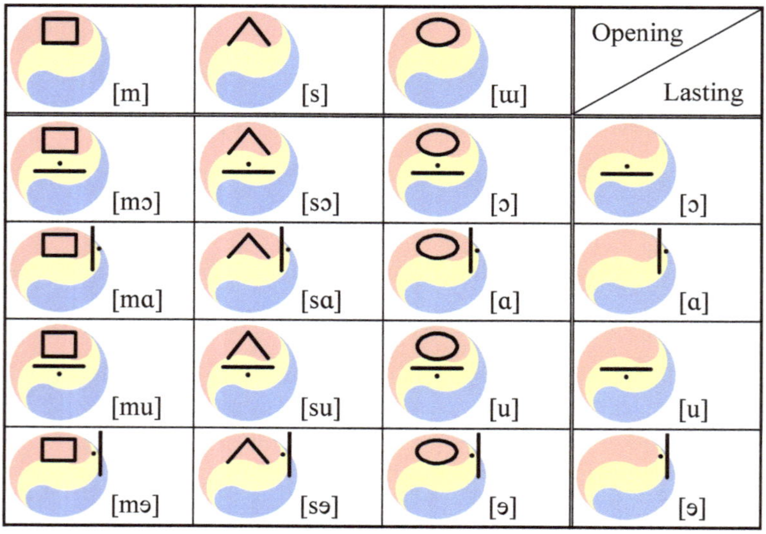

ㅁ [m]	ㅅ [s]	ㅇ [ɯ]	Opening / Lasting
모 [mɔ]	소 [sɔ]	오 [ɔ]	ㅗ [ɔ]
마 [mɑ]	사 [sɑ]	아 [ɑ]	ㅏ [ɑ]
무 [mu]	수 [su]	우 [u]	ㅜ [u]
머 [mə]	서 [sə]	어 [ə]	ㅓ [ə]

The lip puckering and further mouth opening implement the secondary vowel square by the phonetic weight (or feel) and flow. They define [ɔ] and [ɑ] from · [ʌ]; they also define [u] and [ə] from ㅡ [ɯ] (Figure 7a). Acoustically, the soft palate vibrates lightly when we pronounce [ɑ] and [ə] with plain lips. Puckering the lips for [ɔ] and [u], in contrast, increases the relative air pressure in the front side of the oral tract that vibrates the hard palate heavily. This is the reason why we feel heavier for [ɔ] and [u]. The vibrant part of the palate, either soft or hard, defines the active palate.

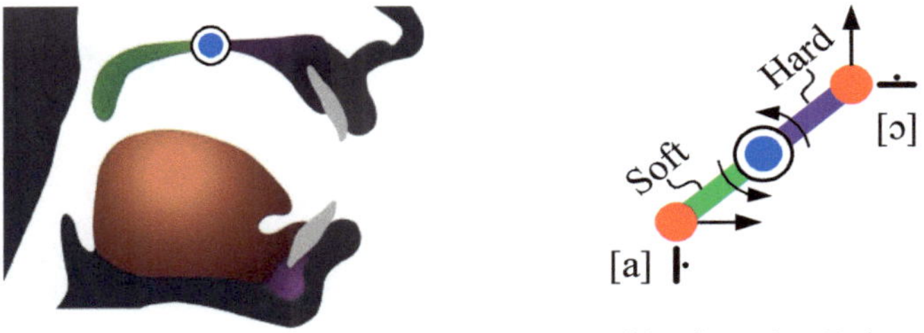

(a) Diverging Mouth (b) Diverging Palate

Figure 17. Diverging Mouth and Palate. (a) Larger mouth opening defines diverging vowels: ㆍ [ʌ], ㅗ [ɔ], and ㅏ [ɑ]. (b) Diverging palate lifts the hard palate and move forward (or rightward) the soft palate simultaneously.

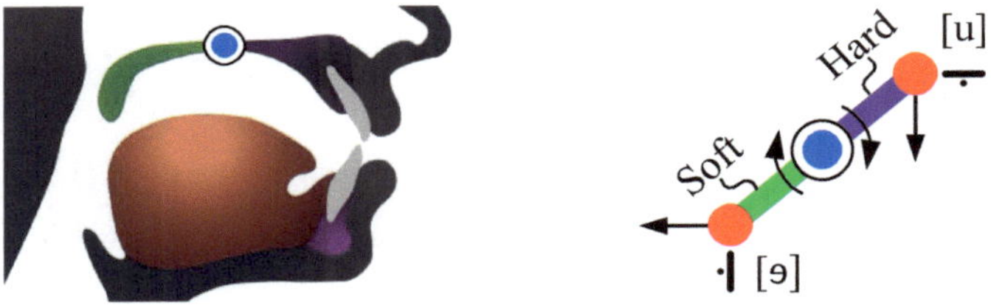

(a) Converging Mouth (b) Converging Palate

Figure 18. Converging Mouth and Palate. (a) Smaller mouth opening defines converging vowels: ㅡ [ɯ], ㅜ [u], and ㅓ [ɘ]. (b) Converging palate lowers the hard palate and moves the soft palate backward (or leftward) simultaneously.

The relative motion of the active palate implements the palatal vowel cross (Figure 16b). Imagine a palatal plane rotating about the palatal center (◉) and horizontally aligned with the lower jaw. If we open the mouth, the soft palate moves forward while the hard palate moves upward in the palatal plane (Figure 17). Conversely, they move the other way if we close the mouth (Figure 18). ㅗ [ɔ] indicates the hard palate moving upward, placing a dot (ㆍ) for the active palate above the reference line (ㅡ). For ㅜ [u], the hard palate moves downward. The soft palate moves forward and backward for ㅏ [ɑ] and ㅓ [ɘ], respectively, using the vertical line (ㅣ).

In summary, we have the seven pictographic vowels: three converging vowels, three diverging vowels, and one independent vowel. The diverging

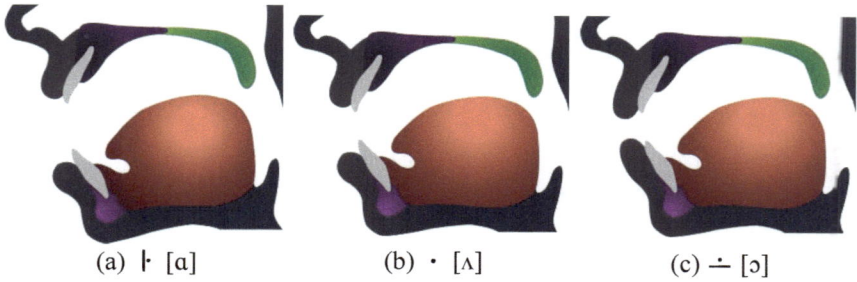

(a) ┠ [ɑ]   (b) · [ʌ]   (c) ᅩ [ɔ]

Figure 19. Diverging Pictographic Vowels. ┠ [ɑ], · [ʌ], and ᅩ [ɔ] give us positive energy with the larger mouth opening.

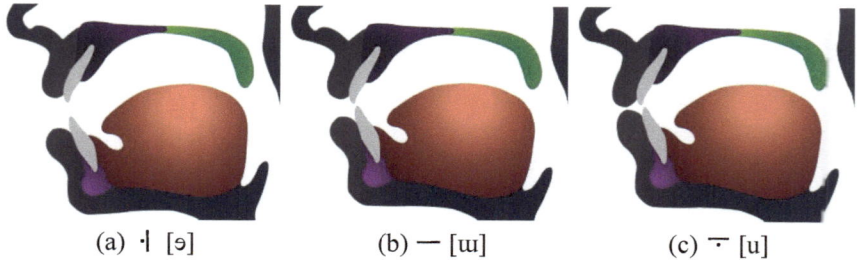

(a) ┤ [ə]   (b) — [ɯ]   (c) ᅮ [u]

Figure 20. Converging Pictographic Vowels. ┤ [ə], — [ɯ], and ᅮ [u] give us negative energy with the smaller mouth opening.

vowels having the larger mouth opening include ┠ [ɑ], · [ʌ], and ᅩ [ɔ] that give us positive energy (Figure 19). The converging vowels having the smaller mouth opening include ┤ [ə], — [ɯ], and ᅮ [u] that give us negative energy (Figure 20). The emotional effects of the converging and diverging vowels go well with those of many Corean native words. The independent vowel ┃ [i] having the tongue back raised is combined with the other vowels front and back to come up with their derivatives.

3.2. Derivative Vowels

Raising the tongue back for ┃ [i], independent of the mouth opening and lip puckering, derives iotized vowels whose letter adds · or ┃ to the base letters. In fact, it triples the number of vowels in the repository (Table 9).

Table 9. Iotized Vowels. (a) The post-iotized derivatives with the raised tongue back add a diacritical line (ㅣ) after the base vowel letters. (b) The pre-iotized derivatives make compound (blended) vowels following the tongue back raised for [j] and add a diacritical dot (•) to base vowel letters.

(a) Post-iotized Vowels | (b) Pre-iotized Vowels

Primitive ㆍ: •, —, ㅣ		Secondary ▣: • + —, ㅣ		Shape/ Weight	Secondary ▣: • + —, ㅣ		Pre-iotized ㅣ+●=●̇	
	ㅣ [i]	ㅏ [ɑ]	ㅓ [ə]	Tall / Light	ㅏ [ɑ]	ㅓ [ə]	ㅑ [jɑ]	ㅕ [jə]
ㆍ [ʌ]	ㅡ [ɯ]	ㅗ [ɔ]	ㅜ [u]	Fat / Heavy	ㅗ [ɔ]	ㅜ [u]	ㅛ [jɔ]	ㅠ [ju]
Post-iotized ●+ㅣ=●ㅣ		ㅐ [æ]	ㅔ [e]	Tall / Light	ㅐ [æ]	ㅔ [e]	ㅒ [jæ]	ㅖ [je]
ㆎ [ɛ]	ㅢ [ɨ]	ㅚ [ø]	ㅟ [y]	Big / Heavy	ㅚ [ø]	ㅟ [y]	[jø]	[jy]
<	>	<	>	Flow	<	>	<	>

First, it turns all pictographic vowels into their post-iotized ones, whose letters add ㅣ to the right of their pictographic bases (Table 9a). Second, the simple vowels with leading ㅣ [i] are the pre-iotized vowels, whose letters add a dot beside the existing dot of their base letters (Table 9b). They are called palatal on-glides with leading [j]. Both the pre-iotized and post-iotized vowels have the same flow and weight of their base vowels.

Articulations of the post-iotized vowels are a little tricky and reduce their discriminability. The raised tongue back modulates the pictographic vowels into their post-iotized ones except ㅣ [i]. Among six post-iotized vowels, diverging ones ㅐ [æ], ㆎ [ɛ], and ㅚ [ø] are derived from ㅏ [ɑ], ㆍ [ʌ], and ㅗ [ɔ], respectively (Figure 21). Converging ones ㅔ [e], ㅢ [ɨ], and ㅟ [y] are derived from ㅓ [ə], ㅡ [ɯ], and ㅜ [u], respectively (Figure 22).

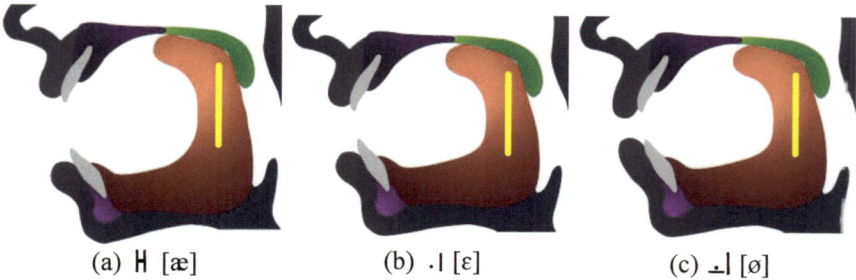

(a) Ⲏ [æ]   (b) ·Ⲓ [ɛ]   (c) ⸖Ⲓ [ø]

Figure 21. Diverging Post-iotized Vowels. Ⲏ [æ], ·Ⲓ [ɛ], and ⸖Ⲓ [ø] raise the tongue back from Ⱶ [ɑ], · [ʌ], and ⸗ [ɔ], respectively.

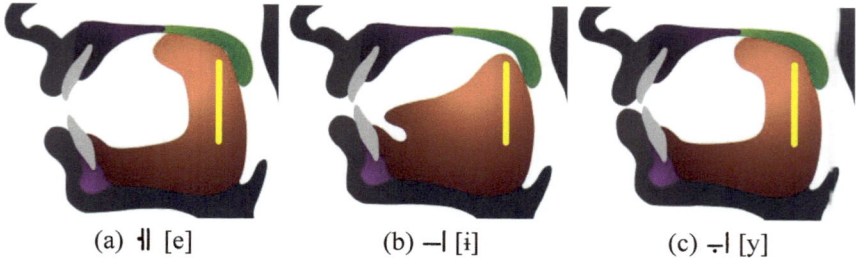

(a) ⵍ [e]   (b) ─Ⲓ [ɨ]   (c) ⸗Ⲓ [y]

Figure 22. Converging Post-iotized Vowels. ⵍ [e], ─Ⲓ [ɨ], and ⸗Ⲓ [y] raise the tongue back from ⵏ [ə], ─ [ɯ], and ⸗ [u], respectively.

However, Ⲏ [æ], ·Ⲓ [ɛ], and ⵍ [e] confuse people due to their similar sounds. The other half ⸖Ⲓ [ø], ─Ⲓ [ɨ], and ⸗Ⲓ [y] are hard to articulate. ⸖Ⲓ [ø] and ⸗Ⲓ [y] need the tongue back raised with the lips puckered (Figures 21c and 22c). ─Ⲓ [ɨ] is the hardest that needs the tongue back raised, keeping the rest flat (Figure 22b). Easier pronunciational variants are ⸖Ⲓ [we], ⸗Ⲓ [wi], and ─Ⲓ [ii]/[e], which are the closest vowels to their simple sounds that end their articulations with the tongue back raised.

Raising the tongue back of the pre-iotized vowels for leading [j] is easier than that of the post-iotized vowels for co-articulating [i]; the pre-iotized vowels add the diacritical dot while the post-iotized ones add the diacritical line. For example, with the vowel ⸚ [jɔ], the composite of Ⲓ [i] and ⸗ [ɔ], we release the raised tongue back for Ⲓ [i] quickly and produce ᅩ [ɔ]. Likewise, ᅣ [ja], ᅲ [ju], and ᅨ [jə] are the pre-iotized versions of ᅡ [a], ᅮ [u], and ᅥ [ə], respectively. For teaching purposes, the pre-iotized vowels of the secondary vowels, instead of the post-iotized vowels, can be introduced first for phonetic and graphic simplicity (Table 10). The rest of the iotized vowels are the post-iotized ones which are created by taking the standard vowel and raising the tongue back. Among all iotized vowels, ᅬ [jø] and ᅱ [jy] are obsolete in the Corean language.

Table 10. Standard Vowels. The standard vowels consist of the primitive, secondary, and pre-iotized vowels.

Primitive ᅡ : •, ─, ᅵ		Secondary ◉ : • + ─, ᅵ		Pre-iotized ᅵ + ● = •●		Shape/ Weight
ᅵ [i]		ᅡ [a]	ᅥ [ə]	ᅣ [ja]	ᅧ [jə]	Tall / Light
• [ʌ]	─ [ɯ]	ᅩ [ɔ]	ᅮ [u]	ᅭ [jɔ]	ᅲ [ju]	Fat / Heavy
<	>	<	>	<	>	Flow

In the 15th century, the post-iotized vowels were double vowels that start from their base vowels and end with [j]. They are called palatal off-glides with ending [j]. In fact, many people still pronounce ─ᅵ as [ɯj].

3.3. Composite Vowels

A composite vowel blends two vowels in harmony whose articulations are close enough to ensure their pronunciational efficiency (Table 11). The composite letter combines the two component letters to form a big letter as its sound forms a complex vowel. For example, ᅪ [wa] is the composite of ᅩ [ɔ] and ᅡ [a] in that we release the puckered lips for ᅩ [ɔ] quickly

Table 11. Composite Vowels. A composite vowel blends vowels in harmony. In other words, a fat vowel in blue is followed by its adjacent tall one in red.

Shape/ Weight	Secondary ⟨•⟩ : • + —, |				Pre-iotized | + ● = •●			
Tall / Light	ㅏ [ɑ]	[wɑ]	ㅓ [ə]	[wə]	ㅑ [jɑ]	[jwjɑ]	ㅕ [jə]	[jwjə]
Fat / Heavy	[ɔ]	[wɑ]	[u]	[wə]	[jɔ]	[jwjɑ]	[ju]	[jwjə]
Tall / Light	[wæ] [æ]		[we] [e]		[jwjæ] [jæ]		[jwje] [je]	
Flow	<	>			<	>		

and open the mouth a little for ㅏ [ɑ]. In terms of articulations, ㅗ [ɔ] and ㅏ [ɑ] are close to [ʌ] so that they all have the same phonetic flow (Figure 7a). Eight composite vowels are possible: ㅘ [wɑ], ㅙ [wæ], ㅝ [wə], ㅞ [we], ㆇ [jwjɑ], ㆈ [jwjæ], ㆊ [jwjə], and ㆋ [jwje]. The first four remain effective while the last four are obsolete.

The vowels in harmony acquire pronunciational efficiency and reduce the movement of their articulators for the composite vowel. The vowels in harmony are a heavy fat vowel and its adjacent light tall vowel in turn. The other order or combinations make their articulations hard. To avoid two letters for a sound, there is a value to keep the post-iotized vowels simple. Otherwise, ㅟ [we] in a compound vowel becomes identical to ㅞ [we], breaking the phonetic design principles and making their letters redundant.

4. Consonant Letters

All consonant letters mutate the basic shapes. The pictographic consonants outline their articulators' shapes. Their blowing derivatives add one or two strokes to the pictographic ones. Double letters denote tense consonants.

4.1. Pictographic Consonants

The pictographic consonants sort into the primitive and secondary ones. The primitive consonants include ㅁ [m], ㅅ [s], and ㅇ [ɯ] that outline the lips, teeth, and throat, respectively, as described in Section 2.2.

The secondary consonants include [n], [l], and [ŋ] whose letters outline the tongue shapes when making their sounds (Figure 23). The letters ㄴ [n], ㄹ [l], and ㅣ [ŋ] characterize the erect tip, bent body, and raised back of the tongue, respectively, that open and close the oral tract. In particular, ㄴ [n] and ㅣ [ŋ] are nasal sounds that have similar phonetic properties with ㅁ [m] as they are graphically close. For ㄹ [l], the air flows over the lateral openings of the elevated tongue blade without the nasal port. ㄹ notably exaggerates the bent curve of the tongue to distinguish it from the others because its derivatives are not used in the Corean language.

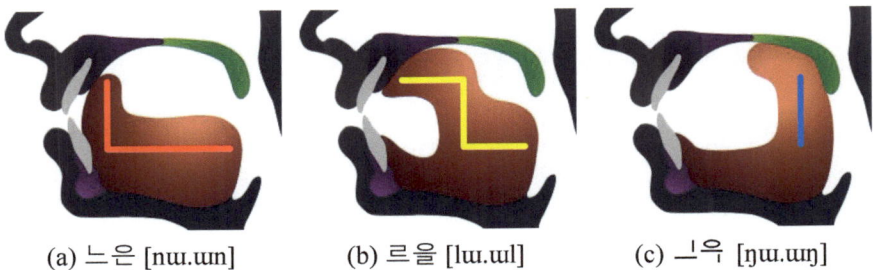

(a) 느은 [nɯ.ɯn]   (b) 르을 [lɯ.ɯl]   (c) ㅣ윽 [ŋɯ.ɯŋ]

Figure 23. Secondary Tongue Consonants. (a) The tip of the tongue touches the upper teeth for ㄴ [n]. (b) The tongue blade touches the upper teeth and the tongue body twists for ㄹ [l]. (c) The tongue back is raised for ㅣ [ŋ].

4.2. Derivative Consonants

The derivative consonants with stronger airflows add one or two strokes to their pictographic letters (Table 12). The sound source with low, mid, and high airflows produces ○ [ɯ], o̅ [ʔ], and o̿ [h], respectively, which fire up the continuant, occlusive, and aspirate sounds. For example, a stop ⊏ [d] adds a stroke to ∟ [n] as [d] is the occlusive version of [n] with mid airflow. A candle-blowing sound ⊨ [t] adds a stroke again to ⊏ [d] as [t] is the aspirate version of [d] with high airflow. Likewise, ∣ [ŋ], ˥ [g], and ㅋ [k]; ∧ [s], ㅈ [z], and ㅊ [ch]; □ [m], ㅂ [b], and ㅍ [p]. Remarkably, ㅂ breaks a line into two pieces and places them on top of □ like horns. ㅍ also breaks two lines into two and puts them beside □ like a double wing. For English readers, [z] and [ch] replace [tɕ] and [tɕʰ] in IPA, respectively.

Table 12. Opening Sounds. The derivative letters add one or two strokes in red to their base letters depending on their airflows. Note that the numbers in parentheses are the numbers of line segments in the pictographs.

ㅍ [pɯ]	ㅊ [chɯ]	⊨ [tɯ]	ㅋ [kɯ]	o̅ [h]	**Aspirate**	
ㅂ [bɯ]	ㅈ [zɯ]	⊏ [dɯ]	˥ [gɯ]	o̅ [ʔ]	**Occlusive**	
□ [mɯ]	∧ [sɯ]	∟ [nɯ]	∣ [ŋɯ]	○ [ɯ]	Continuant	
□ (4)	△ (3)	∟ (2)	∣ (1)	○ (0)	Articulators	Airflow

The reverse articulation of opening sounds, if possible, produces their closing sounds (Table 13). Not all closing sounds are distinguishable, but they all follow three articulatory rules. First, all aspirate closing sounds tail

Table 13. Closing Sounds. Reverse articulation of the opening sounds except throaty ones (○) produce their closing sounds that reuse their letters.

[ɯp] ㅍ	[ɯt] ㅊ	[ɯt] ㅌ	[ɯk] ㅋ	ㅎ	**Aspirate**
[ɯp] ㅂ	[ɯt] ㅈ	[ɯt] ㄷ	[ɯk] ㄱ	ㆆ	**Occlusive**
[ɯm] ㅁ	[ɯt] ㅅ	[ɯn] ㄴ	[ɯŋ] ㅣ	○	Continuant
□ (4)	△ (3)	ㄴ (2)	ㅣ (1)	○ (0)	Airflow Articulators

off their full-blown aspiration, resulting in their occlusive ones. ㅌ [t], for example, has the same closing sound with ㄷ. Second, all toothy closing sounds (△) end up with [t]. Third, all throaty closing sounds (○) are silent or invalid. The consonant table over a rectangular Hundli pattern reminds us of the lax consonants with their names (Table 14).

Table 14. Lax Consonants. The consonant names in Hangul show their versatility even for vertical writing. ㄹ [l] is inserted in its anatomical place.

ㅍ 피읖 [pɯ.ɯp]	ㅊ 치읓 [chɯ.ɯt]	ㅌ 티읕 [tɯ.ɯt]		ㅋ 키읔 [kɯ.ɯk]	ㅎ 히읗 [h]
ㅂ 비읍 [bɯ.ɯp]	ㅈ 지읒 [zɯ.ɯt]	ㄷ 디읃 [dɯ.ɯt]		ㄱ 기윽 [gɯ.ɯk]	ㆆ 이흐 [ʔ]
ㅁ 미음 [mɯ.ɯm]	ㅅ 시읏 [sɯ.ɯt]	ㄴ 니은 [nɯ.ɯn]	ㄹ 리을 [lɯ.ɯl]	ㅣ 이응 [ŋɯ.ɯŋ]	○ 이으 [ɯ]

Remarkably, ㅣ solves the puzzles in ㅣ, ○, and ㆁ, where ㆁ is the old letter whose closing sound is only known as [ŋ]. The tongue back produces the pictographic vowel ㅣ [i] and consonant ㅣ [ŋ] with its erect sides so that their letters are graphically similar. Phonetically, the opening ㅣ [ŋ] and ○ [ɯ] are similar as their articulators are close. The closing ㅣ [ŋ] and ㆁ [ŋ] are the same, and so are their opening sounds. Originally, ㆁ might attach ○ below ㅣ to distinguish ㅣ from ㅣ and consider the similar sounds of ㅣ and ○ in the pictographic principle. Since the opening ㆁ [ŋ] became ○ [ɯ] or obsolete in the Corean orthography, ○ void of the closing sound replaced ㆁ by their phonetic and graphic similarities.

4.3. Composite Consonants

Homogeneous digraphs or double letters represent tense consonant sounds by putting their base letters side by side. To produce a "tense" sound, take any lax sound and increase the glottal tension. For example, ㄲ [ˀgɯ.ɯk] denotes the tense sound of ㄱ. Among all tense sounds, only five are effective in the Corean orthography: ㅃ [ˀbɯ.ɯp], ㅆ [ˀsɯ.ɯt], ㅉ [ˀzɯ.ɯt], ㄸ [ˀdɯ.ɯt], and ㄲ [ˀgɯ.ɯk].

Consonant compounds blending two different consonant sounds are not allowed in the Corean language. Some heterogeneous digraphs of two different consonant letters are used only in the closing position for the Corean orthography, giving better hints to word roots: ㄳ, ㄵ, ㄶ, ㄺ, ㄻ, ㄼ, ㄽ, ㄾ, ㄿ, ㅀ, and ㅄ. In general, the first letter makes the closing sound of the syllable while the second one carries over its opening sound to the next syllable if any. Yet in some cases of ㄺ, ㄻ, and ㄿ, the first letter, ㄹ, clues us in the word roots and the second letter takes the closing sound of the syllable.

5. Hangul Wing

Congratulations for mastering 한글! 한글윙 recapitulates both letters and syllables (Figure 25). The primitive vowel letters outline their articulators (Figure 24a). The pictographic and derivative vowels are listed in the 4x6 matrix (Figure 25a). The pictographic consonant letters are aligned well with their vocal valves (Figure 24b). Twice differentiable lax consonants are listed in the 3x5 matrix (Figure 25b). The letter names exemplify their speech sounds and typographic changes in a syllabic block. Note that a dot in a vowel letter is replaced by a short line for easy writing. The disyllabic names are contractible to the monosyllable ones. For example, 음 for ㅁ, 는 for ㄴ, 를 for ㄹ, 읍 for ㅂ, 윽 for ㄱ, etc.

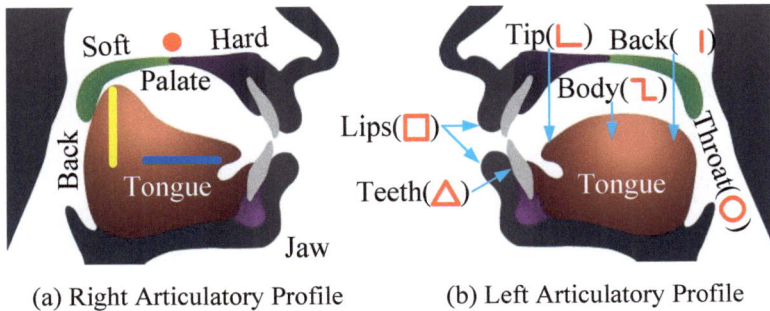

(a) Right Articulatory Profile   (b) Left Articulatory Profile

Figure 24. Articulatory Profiles. (a) Vowel articulators include the palate, flat tongue, and tongue back. (b) Vocal valves including the lips, teeth, and tongue control the sound source from the throat.

Here are some useful expressions in Corean: 예 – Yes, 아니오 – No, 안녕하세요 – Hello, 안녕하세요? – How are you? 사랑해요 – I love you, 고마워요 – Thank you, 한국 – Corea, 밥 – meal / rice, 물 – water, 말 – language, 노래 – song, 친구 – friend, 미안해요 – I'm sorry, 잠시만요 – Just a moment / Excuse me, and 얼마예요? – How much is it?

(a) Vowel Table

	Primitive	Post-iotized	Secondary	Pre-iotized
(formula)	+ ∶ · , ㅡ , ㅣ	● · ㅣ+●=●	● ∶ · + ㅣ , ㅡ , ㅣ	● ㅣ+●=●
	·ㅇ	ㅇ	ㆍ / ㅏ	ㅗ / ㅛ	ㅗ / ㅛ
	·ㅡ	ㅡ	ㅗ / ㅜ	ㅐ / ㅔ	ㅒ / ㅖ
	·ㅣ	ㅣ	ㅘ / ㅝ	ㅙ / ㅞ	ㅚ / ㅟ

(b) Consonant Table

Articulators \ Airflow	Continuant	Occlusive	Aspirate
□	ㅁ 미음	ㅂ 비읍	ㅍ 피읖
△	ㅅ 시옷	ㅈ 지읒	ㅊ 치읓
∟	ㄴ 니은	ㄷ 디귿	ㅌ 티읕
|	ㄱ 기역	ㅋ 키읔	ㅇ 이
○	ㅇ 이응		ㅎ 히읗

| ㄹ 리을 |
| ㅇ 이응 |

Figure 25. Hangul Wing. Its name in the fuselage illustrates three typical syllables in Hangul. Vowel and consonant letters are organized in the left and right wings to cubistically show their structures and articulatory features. (a) Pictographic and derivative vowels are listed in a 4x6 matrix with their names. A composite vowel forms a big vowel as its sound forms a complex vowel in harmony, that is, a leading fat vowel followed by its adjacent tall vowel. For example, ㅘ [wa] is the composite of ㅗ [ɔ] and ㅏ [a]. Likewise, ㅙ [wæ], ㅝ [wɔ], and ㅞ [we] are composite vowels. (b) The pictographic and derivative consonants are listed in a 3x5 matrix with their names. Homogeneous digraphs represent tense consonants. For example, ㄲ [ˀku.uk] denotes the tense sound of ㄱ [gu.uk]. Likewise, ㅃ [ˀbu.up], ㅆ [ˀsu.ut], ㅉ [ˀzu.ut], and ㄸ [ˀdu.ut] are tesned consonants.